Healthy Baking

Dairy-Free, Gluten-Free, Sugar-Free Baking Cookbook

DEDICATION

Contents

Gluten-Free Baking Recipes

Gluten-Free Chilli Cornbread

PREP: 20 MINS

COOK: 30 MINS

plus at least 2 hrs soaking

SERVES 4 – 6

Ingredients

200g polenta or fine ground cornmeal

284ml pot buttermilk

25g butter

1 red chilli, deseeded and finely chopped

1 tsp baking powder

 (look for a gluten-free one)

¼ tsp bicarbonate of soda

50g frozen sweetcorn, defrosted

2 large eggs, beaten

Method

1. Lightly toast the polenta in a dry frying pan for 3-4 mins, stirring to ensure even cooking, until the polenta has heated through, is fragrant and small patches are starting to turn golden brown. Take off the heat, tip half into a large bowl and add the buttermilk. Stir well, cover and leave to soak for 2-3 hrs.

2. Melt the butter in a 25cm ovenproof frying pan (a cast-iron one is perfect) and heat oven to 220C/200C fan/gas 7. Stir the butter and the remaining ingredients, including the rest of the toasted polenta and 1/2 tsp salt, into the buttermilk and polenta mixture. (Don't wipe out the frying pan – the slick of butter will ensure the bread doesn't stick.)

3. Put the pan back on the heat and turn up the temperature. Pour the mixture into the pan – it should sizzle as it hits it, like a Yorkshire pudding. Put the whole pan in the oven and bake for 15-20 mins until golden brown and firm in the middle. Leave to cool a little, then serve cut into wedges.

Peanut Butter Cookies

PREP: 15 MINS

COOK: 12 MINS

EASY

MAKES 16

Ingredients

200g peanut butter (crunchy or smooth is fine)

175g golden caster sugar

¼ tsp fine table salt

1 large egg

Method

1. Heat oven to 180C/160C fan/gas 4 and line 2 large baking trays with baking parchment.

2. Measure the peanut butter and sugar into a bowl. Add ¼ tsp fine table salt and mix well with a wooden spoon. Add the egg and mix again until the mixture forms a dough.

3. Break off cherry tomato sized chunks of dough and place, well spaced apart, on the trays. Press the cookies down with the back of a fork to squash them a little. The cookies can now be frozen for 2 months, cook from frozen adding an extra min or 2 to the cooking time.

4. Bake for 12 mins, until golden around the edges and paler in the centre. Cool on the trays for 10 mins, then transfer to a wire rack and cool completely. Store in a cookie jar for up to 3 days.

Pastel De Choclo - Corn Cake

PREP: 15 MINS

COOK: 1 HR, 45 MINS

MORE EFFORT

SERVES 4

Ingredients

2 large eggs

500g frozen sweetcorn, defrosted

75g butter, melted and cooled

2 tsp cornflour

1½ tbsp baking powder

1 tbsp granulated sugar

oil, for greasing

100g feta, cut into small cubes

25g Botija Peruvian or Kalamata olives, sliced

Method

1. Heat oven to 120C/100C fan/gas 1/2. Grease a 20 x 20cm cake tin and line with baking parchment. Separate the eggs. Put the yolks in a food processor or blender with the sweetcorn and blitz to a rough purée. Tip the blended mixture into a large bowl and stir in the butter, cornflour, baking powder, sugar and 1/2 tsp salt. Mix thoroughly.

2. Whisk the egg whites until they have reached the stiff peak stage. Gently fold the egg whites into the corn mixture using a large metal spoon until completely incorporated, keeping as much air in the mixture as possible.

3. Spread the corn batter over the base of the tin with a spatula. Sprinkle over the cubes of cheese and push them into the mixture so they are almost completely covered.

4. Cook for 1 hr 45 mins until firm and golden and shrinking slightly from the sides. Remove from the oven and leave to cool for at least 15 mins before cutting into chunks and serving, scattered with olives. Leftovers will keep in the fridge until the next day.

Gluten-Free Banana Bread

PREP: 10 MINS

COOK: 1 HR, 15 MINS

EASY

SERVES 8

Ingredients

5 small ripe bananas (4 mashed, 1 sliced down the middle to decorate the top)

150g gluten-free self-raising flour

100g gluten-free oats

50g ground almonds

1 tsp gluten-free baking powder

1 tsp cinnamon

90g dark brown sugar

90g caster sugar

100g butter, melted

2 large eggs, beaten

1 tbsp icing sugar

Method

1. Heat the oven to 180C/160C fan/gas 4 and line a 900g loaf tin with parchment paper (our tin was 19 x 9 x 6cm). Put all the ingredients, except the sliced banana, 1 tbsp caster sugar and the icing sugar, into a large bowl and stir until smooth and combined.

2. Pour into the tin and put the two remaining banana halves cut-side up across the top of the batter, pressing down slightly. Sprinkle over the caster sugar. Bake for 1hr-1hr 15 mins until a skewer comes out clean, covering with foil towards the end of cooking if it browns too much.

3. Dust with icing sugar and leave to cool.

Easy Flatbread

PREP: 10 MINS

COOK: 10 MINS

EASY

MAKES 8

Ingredients

400g gluten-free self-raising flour, plus extra for dusting (we used Doves)

1 tbsp cumin seeds, toasted

300ml natural yogurt

Method

1. Heat the grill to medium and dust a baking sheet with a little flour. Mix the flour and cumin seeds in a bowl, then season. Stir in the yogurt and 100ml water, then mix well to form a soft dough.

2. Divide the dough into 8 equal pieces, then shape into circles or ovals about ½cm thick. Dust lightly with a little flour. Grill on the baking sheet for 3-5 mins on each side until golden and puffed. Serve warm.

Amaretto Meringue Cake With Strawberries & Cherries

PREP: 30 MINS

COOK: 1 HR

plus cooling

MORE EFFORT

SERVES 12 – 15

Ingredients

400g strawberries, hulled then halved or quartered (save a few whole with stalks on, to serve)

400g cherries, halved and pitted (save a few whole with stalks on, to serve)

50g icing sugar, plus 1 tbsp

600ml pot double cream

50ml amaretto

½ tsp almond extract

For the meringues

6 large egg whites

300g white caster sugar

¾ tsp white wine vinegar

100g flaked toasted almonds

Method

1. Heat oven to 140C/120C fan/gas 1 and cut 3 pieces of baking parchment to fit 3 baking sheets for the meringues (if you don't have 3 baking sheets, you can cook it in batches – simply divide the meringue mixture into 3 and cook separately). Using a plate

or the base of a cake tin, draw a 20cm circle on each piece of parchment, then flip over so that the pencil side is facing down. Put 3 oven racks in your oven – if you only have 2 but have a large grill pan, this will work too, sat in the bottom of the oven.

2. Put the egg whites in a large bowl, and whisk with an electric hand whisk until thick and holding soft peaks. Start adding the sugar, 1 or 2 tbsp at a time, whisking continuously. When all the sugar has been incorporated, the meringue should be thick, glossy and holding stiff peaks. Add the vinegar and whisk again briefly. Use a blob of meringue to stick down the corners of each piece of parchment to the trays. Divide the meringue between the 3 circles on the parchment, swirling it towards the outline to make thin circles. Scatter the almonds over, saving a few to serve on top once assembled. Bake for 1 hr, then leave to cool in the oven.

3. When the oven is completely cold, remove the meringues and place somewhere cool and dry for up to 24 hrs, or assemble straight away. Toss the fruit with 1 tbsp icing sugar and set aside to macerate for 10-15 mins. Pour the cream, amaretto, almond extract and remaining icing sugar into a large bowl, and whisk until softly whipped. Use a little of the cream to stick your least successful meringue to a cake stand or plate. Spread over a third of the cream and scatter with some strawberries

and cherries. Top with the remaining meringues, cream and fruit, finishing the top layer with the whole strawberries and cherries. Scatter over the remaining almonds and serve. Leftovers will keep in the fridge for 1 day.

Walnut Seed Loaf

PREP: 25 MINS

COOK: 30 MINS

plus rising

EASY

CUTS INTO 12 THICK SLICES

Ingredients

100g cornflour

300g gluten-free brown bread flour

(we used Doves Farm)

2 tbsp soya flour

85g potato starch

2 tsp xanthan gum

7g sachet easy-bake dried yeast

1 tbsp caster sugar

450ml milk, warmed to hand temperature

2 tbsp sunflower oil, plus extra for greasing

1 tbsp white wine vinegar

100g mixed seed (we used linseeds, hemp seeds, pumpkin seeds and sesame seeds)

50g walnut, roughly chopped

Method

1. Mix the flours, potato starch, xanthan gum, yeast, sugar and 1½ tsp salt in a large bowl. Mix together the milk, oil and vinegar in a separate bowl, then add to the dry ingredients and mix until a soft dough comes together. Cover loosely with oiled cling film

and leave to rise in a warm place for 1 hr.

2. Knead in most of the seeds and walnuts. Shape into a large round – oiled hands will help. Roll the round in the remaining seeds and nuts, then lift onto a baking tray. Loosely cover again with oiled cling film and leave for 1 hr more.

3. Heat oven to 220C/200C fan/gas 7. Bake the bread for 15 mins, then reduce oven to 190C/170C fan/gas 5 and continue baking for 30 mins until the loaf sounds hollow when tapped on the base. Leave on a wire rack to cool, wrapped in a clean tea towel – this will help to keep the loaf soft.

Buttermilk & Sultana Scones

PREP: 20 MINS

COOK: 10 MINS - 12 MINS

EASY

MAKES 8

Ingredients

450g gluten-free self-raising flour blend, plus extra for sprinkling

1 tbsp gluten-free baking powder

2 tsp xanthan gum

85g golden caster sugar, plus extra for sprinkling

100g butter, diced

50g sultana, plumped up in boiling water for 10 mins, then drained

284ml pot buttermilk

100ml milk, plus extra for brushing

butter and jam, or clotted cream and strawberries (optional), to serve

Method

1. Heat oven to 220C/200C fan/gas 7 and lightly flour a large baking sheet. Tip the flour into a large bowl and stir in the baking powder, xanthan gum, sugar and ½ tsp salt.

2. Rub the butter into the flour mixture with your fingertips until it is completely incorporated, then add the sultanas. Stir the buttermilk and milk together, then pour into the flour mixture. Stir in with the blade of a knife to make a soft dough.

3. Tip onto a lightly floured work surface and pat out with your hands until about 4cm thick. Don't knead the mixture as this will make a heavy scone, and if the mixture seems a little too wet, leave for a few mins, as gluten-free flour requires more liquid than wheat flour. Stamp out rounds using a 7cm floured

cutter, then place the scones on the baking tray, spaced apart. You will need to lightly squash the dough trimmings together to give you 8-9 scones in total. Brush the tops of the scones with milk, sprinkle with sugar and bake for 10-12 mins until pale golden. Serve with butter and jam, or push the boat out with clotted cream and strawberries, too. Best eaten on the day they are made.

Dairy-Free Cake Recipes

Carrot Cake

PREP: 1 HR - 1 HR, 15 MINS

EASY

15 SLICES

Ingredients

175g light muscovado sugar

175ml sunflower oil

3 large eggs, lightly beaten

140g grated carrot (about 3 medium)

100g raisins

grated zest of 1 large orange

175g self-raising flour

1 tsp bicarbonate of soda

1 tsp ground cinnamon

½ tsp grated nutmeg (freshly grated will give you the best flavour)

For the frosting

175g icing sugar

1½-2 tbsp orange juice

Method

1. Heat the oven to 180C/fan160C/gas 4. Oil and line the base and sides of an 18cm square cake tin with baking parchment.

2. Tip 175g light muscovado sugar, 175ml sunflower oil and 3 large beaten eggs into a big mixing bowl. Lightly mix with a wooden spoon. Stir in 140g grated carrots, 100g raisins and grated zest of 1 large orange.

3. Sift 175g self-raising flour, 1 tsp bicarbonate of soda, 1 tsp ground cinnamon and ½ tsp grated nutmeg into the bowl. Mix everything together, the mixture will be soft and almost runny.

4. Pour the mixture into the prepared tin and bake for 40-45 mins or until it feels firm and springy when you press it in the centre.

5. Cool in the tin for 5 mins, then turn it out, peel off the paper and cool on a wire rack. (You can freeze the cake at this point if you want to serve it at a later date.)

6. Beat 175g icing sugar and 1½ - 2 tbsp orange juice in a small bowl until smooth – you want the icing about as runny as single cream.

7. Put the cake on a serving plate and boldly drizzle the icing back and forth in diagonal lines over the top, letting it drip down the sides.

Blueberry & Coconut Cake

PREP: 20 MINS

COOK: 1 HR - 1 HR, 15 MINS

EASY

SERVES 12

Ingredients

250ml rice

bran oil, plus extra for the tin

3 eggs

225g caster sugar

2 tsp vanilla extract

300g self-raising flour

50g desiccated coconut

175ml soya milk

140g fresh or frozen blueberries, plus extra to serve

icing sugar, to dust

Method

1. Heat oven to 180C/160C fan/gas 4 and grease a 22cm Bundt or ring tin. Whisk the oil, eggs, sugar and vanilla in a large bowl. Combine the flour and coconut. Alternately, fold the flour mix and soya milk into the wet ingredients, starting and ending with the flour.

2. Spoon a quarter into the tin. Fold the blueberries into the remaining batter, then spoon into the tin. Bake for 1-1¼ hrs, or until a skewer comes out clean. Cover the cake with foil if it browns too quickly.

3. Cool in tin for 10 mins, then turn out onto a wire rack and cool completely. Fill centre of the cake with extra blueberries and dust with icing sugar to serve.

Vegan Sponge Cake

PREP: 20 MINS

COOK: 30 MINS - 35 MINS

EASY

SERVES 8 – 10

Ingredients

150g dairy-free spread, plus extra for the tins

300ml dairy-free milk, we used oat milk

1 tbsp cider vinegar

28

1 vanilla pod, seeds scraped

300g self-raising flour

200g golden caster sugar

1 tsp bicarbonate of soda

For the filling

100g dairy-free spread

200g icing sugar, plus extra for dusting

4 tbsp jam, we used strawberry

Method

1. Heat oven to 180C/160C fan/gas 4. Line the bases of 2 x 20cm sandwich tins with baking parchment and grease with a little of the dairy-free spread.
2. Put the dairy-free milk into a jug and add the vinegar, leave for a few minutes until it looks a little lumpy. Put half of the vanilla seeds and all the other cake ingredients into a large bowl then pour over the milk mixture. Using electric beaters or a wooden spoon, beat everything together until smooth.
3. Divide the mix between your two tins then bake in the centre of the oven for 30-35 mins or until a skewer inserted into the

middle of the cakes comes out cleanly. Leave them in their tins until cool enough to handle then carefully turn out onto wire racks to cool completely.

4. While the cakes are cooling, make the filling. To make the vegan buttercream, whisk or beat together the dairy-free spread, icing sugar and remaining vanilla seeds until pale and fluffy. Dairy-free spreads do vary so if the spread you are using is quite soft try to avoid using electric beaters. Stir the ingredients together instead to avoid overworking it. However, if the mixture is too firm, use electric beaters to help lighten it and add 1-2 tbsp of dairy-free milk when whisking.

5. Spread the jam onto one of the cooled sponges, top with the buttercream then place the other sponge on top. Dust the assembled cake with a little icing sugar or caster sugar before slicing.

Choc-Cherry Fudge Torte With Cherry Sorbet

PREP: 25 MINS

COOK: 45 MINS

plus soaking

MORE EFFORT

CUTS INTO 10 SLICES

Ingredients

100g dried sour cherry

5 tbsp brandy

300g gluten- and wheat-free plain flour (we used Doves Farm)

85g cocoa, plus extra for dusting

200g light soft brown sugar

1 tsp gluten-free baking powder

1 tsp gluten-free bicarbonate of soda

1 tsp xanthan gum

150ml sunflower oil

350ml rice milk (preferably unsweetened)

150ml agave syrup

a little icing sugar, for dusting

For the sorbet

2 x 600g jars cherry compote

200g caster sugar

Method

1. For the sorbet, whizz the compote with the sugar until smooth-

ish, then tip into a freezer-proof container. Freeze until solid.

2. Mix the cherries and the brandy and leave to soak for a few hrs.

3. Heat oven to 160C/140C fan/gas 3. Line the base of a round, 20cm loosebottomed tin with baking parchment. Mix the flour, cocoa, brown sugar, baking powder, bicarb and xanthan gum in a big bowl. Whisk the oil, rice milk and agave syrup, then add to the dry ingredients and stir in with a wooden spoon. Add the cherries and any brandy, then scrape into the tin. Bake for 35-45 mins until crisp on top but fudgy in the centre. Cool in the tin.

4. Carefully lift the torte onto a serving plate. Dust with cocoa and icing sugar, and serve with the cherry sorbet.

Gingered Rich Fruit Cake

PREP: 30 MINS

COOK: 2 HRS - 2 HRS, 30 MINS

plus 15 mins to decorate

EASY

SERVES 10 – 12

Ingredients

oil, for greasing

100g each dried currant, sultanas and raisins

225g each semi-dried fig and prunes, roughly chopped

200g tub crystallised ginger

100g stem ginger, from a jar, chopped

2 tbsp stem ginger syrup

4 tbsp Cointreau

1 tsp each ground ginger

 and mixed spice

zest 2 lemons

150ml olive oil

175g light muscovado sugar

4 eggs

225g gluten-free flour

1 tsp gluten-free baking powder

For the topping

4 tbsp apricot jam

1 tbsp Cointreau

450g mixed fruit, including figs, prunes, date and apricots

Method

1. Heat oven to 140C/fan 120C/gas 1. Lightly oil a 71/2cm deep, 25cm round cake tin, and line it with a double layer of baking parchment.

2. Mix the dried fruits, ginger and syrup, Cointreau, spices and lemon zest. Put the olive oil, sugar and eggs in a bowl, whisk together until light and fluffy. Sift the flour and baking powder into the mixture and tip in the fruit. Fold and stir together well.

3. Spoon the mixture into the cake tin. Bake in the centre of the oven for 2-21/2 hrs, or until a skewer inserted into the centre comes out clean. Cover with foil if the cake begins to over-brown. Take from the oven and leave to cool in the tin. Remove, leaving the baking parchment in place until you decorate.

4. For the topping: warm the jam and Cointreau together until the jam is liquid, allow to cool. Arrange the fruit on the cake and brush with the jam.

Chocolate, Orange & Hazelnut Cake

PREP: 50 MINS

COOK: 50 MINS

plus 8 hrs drying

MORE EFFORT

SERVES 10

Ingredients

175ml light-coloured olive oil, plus extra for greasing

140g blanched hazelnuts

100ml orange juice, plus zest 1 orange

140g self-raising flour

½ tsp baking powder

50g cocoa powder

3 large eggs

175g light brown muscovado sugar

For the candied orange slices

300g golden caster sugar

1 large orange, cut into 3mm/1/8in slices

To decorate

75ml orange juice

100g dairy-free dark chocolate

50g blanched hazelnuts, toasted

1 tsp edible gold powder (see tip)

Method

1. Make the candied orange slices a day ahead if you can. Put the sugar and 300ml water in a medium saucepan and bring to the boil. Reduce to a gentle simmer, add the orange slices and cook for 1 hr-1 hr 10 mins or until the pith is translucent, turning occasionally. Line a baking tray with parchment. Carefully remove the slices from the syrup, place on the prepared tray and set aside to dry (at least 8 hrs) before cutting in half. Reserve the syrup.

2. Heat oven to 180C/160C fan/gas 4. Lightly grease a loaf tin (mine was 900g) with olive oil and line with a strip of baking parchment.

3. Grind the hazelnuts in a food processor until they resemble coarse breadcrumbs (do not blitz them too much or they will become oily), then add to a bowl along with the orange zest, a pinch of salt and the flour, baking powder and cocoa. Mix together until evenly combined.

4. Pour the oil and the orange juice into a jug and mix together. Put the eggs and sugar in a tabletop mixer or large bowl and whisk together for 5-10 mins or until the mixture has tripled in volume and holds a ribbon on the surface when the beaters are lifted out. Slowly pour the oil mixture into the egg mixture and

fold together until combined.

5. Add the flour mixture to the egg mixture in 3 or 4 additions, folding together until combined. You can't sieve this mixture over the eggs because of the hazelnuts, but try not to dump the flour in one place – you need to be careful and fold the batter to retain its lightness. Once fully combined, pour the batter into the prepared loaf tin and bake for 50-55 mins or until a skewer inserted into the centre of the cake comes out clean.

6. Prick the top of the cake all over, then pour over 5 tbsp of the reserved orange syrup. Cool in the tin for 15 mins, then turn out onto a wire rack to cool completely. Trim the top of the cake (keep this for a mini trifle) and turn out, cut-side down, onto a serving platter.

7. To decorate, pour the orange juice into a small pan and bring to a simmer. Put the chocolate in a small bowl, pour the orange juice over and stir together to form a smooth ganache. Set aside in the fridge until thickened, about 20-25 mins. Tip the hazelnuts into a small bowl and add the gold powder with a dash of water, stirring together to coat. Put the ganache in a piping bag fitted with a small round piping tip. Pipe in peaks over the top of the cake, decorating with the golden hazelnuts and the orange slices. Will keep for up to 3 days in an airtight container.

Better Beetroot Brownies

PREP: 15 MINS

COOK: 40 MINS - 45 MINS

EASY

SERVES 12

Ingredients

500g whole raw beetroot, washed

100ml rapeseed oil

250g good-quality dark chocolate

(70% cocoa, dairy-free if you want, chopped)

3 large eggs

200g golden caster sugar

2 tsp vanilla extract

140g plain flour

75g cocoa powder

1 tsp baking powder

50g walnut piece, roughly chopped

For the icing

100g icing sugar

1 tbsp beetroot juice

Method

1. Heat oven to 180C/160C fan/gas 4. Grease and line a 20 x 30cm cake tin with baking parchment. Boil the beetroots in a pan of boiling salted water for 15-20 mins or until tender. Drain and leave to cool before peeling (wear clean rubber gloves to peel if you want to avoid beet-stained hands). Chop one-third of the cooked beetroots into small cubes and blitz the

remainder in a blender or food processor to a paste. Sit the paste in a sieve over a bowl – just until you have collected 1-2 tbsp juice. Save this for the icing, and mix the oil into the purée.

2. Melt the chocolate slowly in a heatproof bowl over a pan of barely simmering water and leave to cool slightly. Use an electric whisk to beat the eggs, sugar and vanilla together in a large mixing bowl until light, fluffy and tripled in size. Carefully fold the eggs into the beetroot mixture, followed by the melted chocolate. Fold in the flour, cocoa powder and baking powder, then add walnuts and the chopped beetroot.

3. Pour into your prepared tin and bake for 20-25 mins. The brownies should still be slightly gooey in the middle. Allow to cool. Mix enough reserved beetroot juice with the icing sugar to get a runny icing – dilute with water if you need. Remove brownies from the tin, drizzle with the icing and cut into squares.

Vegan Cupcakes

PREP: 30 MINS

COOK: 20 MINS

EASY

MAKES 12

Ingredients

150ml almond or soy milk

½ tsp cider vinegar

110g vegan butter or sunflower spread

110g caster sugar

1 tsp vanilla extract

110g self-raising flour

½ tsp baking powder

For the buttercream

125g vegan butter

250g icing sugar

1¼ tsp vanilla extract

a few drops of vegan food colourings (check the label)

Method

1. Heat the oven to 180C/160C fan/gas 4. Line the holes of a 12-hole cupcake tin with paper cases. Stir the milk and vinegar in a jug and leave to thicken slightly for a few mins.

2. Beat the butter and sugar with an electric whisk until well combined. Whisk in the vanilla, then add the milk a splash at a time, alternating with spoonfuls of the flour. Fold in any remaining flour, the baking powder and a pinch of salt until you get a creamy batter. Don't worry if it looks a little curdled at this stage.

3. Divide between the cupcake cases, filling them two-thirds full, and bake for 20 - 25 mins until golden and risen. Leave to cool on a wire rack.

4. To make the buttercream, beat the butter, icing sugar and vanilla with an electric whisk until pale and creamy. Divide between bowls and colour with different food colourings until you get desired strength. Spoon or pipe onto the cooled cupcakes.

Sugar-Free Baking Recipes

Sugar-Free Lemon Drizzle Cake

PREP: 10 MINS

COOK: 1 HR - 1 HR, 10 MINS

EASY

CUTS INTO 8-10 SLICES

Ingredients

225g self-raising flour, sifted

½ tsp baking powder

225g xylitol

2 lemons, zest only

2 large eggs, at room temperature

125ml sunflower oil

1 tbsp milk

200g 0% fat Greek yogurt

Drizzle

1 lemon, juice only

50g xylitol

Method

1. Preheat the oven to 180C/ 160C fan/ Gas 4. Grease and line a 1.2 litre loaf tin (22cm x 13cm width, 7cm depth) with baking parchment. Mix together the flour, baking powder, xylitol and lemon zest in a large bowl.
2. Mix the eggs, sunflower oil, milk and yoghurt together in a separate bowl or jug and stir them into the flour mixture.
3. Spoon into a tin and smooth the surface. Transfer to the oven immediately, bake on the middle shelf of the oven for 1 hour –

1 hour 10 mins. Check after 50 mins, if the cake is becoming too dark, cover loosely with foil.

4. Just before the end of cooking time, make the drizzle by heating the lemon juice and xylitol. Stir over a low heat until the xylitol has dissolved. Once the cake is cooked, take it out of the oven and pour over the drizzle.

5. Cool in the tin before turning it out.

Sugar-Free Brownie

INGREDIENTS

425g can black beans, drained, rinsed

12 fresh dates, pitted

1/4 cup coconut oil

1/4 cup milk

1 teaspoon vanilla bean paste

1/2 cup raw cacao

1 tablespoon walnuts, halved

1 tablespoon pistachios

1 tablespoon hazelnuts, halved

Select all ingredients

EQUIPMENT

16cm x 26cm baking tin

METHOD

1. Preheat oven to 180C or 160C fan-forced. Grease and line base and sides of a 16cm X 26cm baking tin with baking paper.

2. Process beans until smooth, scraping down sides of bowl several times (this will take 1-2 minutes). Add dates, oil, milk and vanilla and process until smooth. Add cacao and process until combined. Spoon into prepared tin and level surface with a spatula.

3. Arrange nuts on top in 16 clusters (imagine how you will cut brownie once cooked). Bake for 20 minutes or until top forms a crust. Cool in pan. Cut into 16 rectangles.

Sugar-Free Banana Bread

INGREDIENTS

4 very ripe bananas

2 eggs

1/2 cup olive oil

1/4 cup milk

1 teaspoon vanilla bean paste

1 teaspoon Ground Cinnamon

1 cup wholemeal flour

1 cup plain flour

1 teaspoon baking powder

1 teaspoon bicarbonate of soda

Pinch salt

EQUIPMENT

11.5cm x 22cm loaf pan

METHOD

1. Preheat the oven to 160C or 140C fan-force. Grease and line an 11.5cm x 22cm (base measurements) loaf pan with baking paper.

2. Mash bananas in a large bowl with a fork until smooth. Add eggs, oil, milk and vanilla and stir until combined. Sift flours, cinnamon, baking powder, bicarbonate and salt over banana mixture (tip in the flour kernels). Stir until combined. Spoon into prepared pan and level top with a spatula. Bake for 1 hour 10 minutes or until a skewer inserted in centre comes out clean. Stand in pan for 5 minutes. Transfer to a wire rack to cool.

Louise's Flourless Chocolate Biscuits

INGREDIENTS

110g (3/4 cup) raw cashews, or roasted cashews

110g (3/4 cup) macadamias

30g (1/4 cup) MasterFoods® Sesame Seeds

225g (1 1/2 cups) fresh dates, pitted

1 1/2 tablespoons raw cacao powder (or cocoa powder)

EQUIPMENT

Food processor

METHOD

1. Preheat oven to 170C/150C fan forced. Line 2 baking trays with baking paper. Place all ingredients in a food processor and process for 1 minute or until the nuts are finely chopped and the mixture is well combined and smooth.

2. Roll 2 teaspoonfuls of mixture into a ball. Place on prepared tray. Repeat with the remaining mixture to make about 30 balls. Use a fork to flatten slightly. Bake for 10-12 minutes until lightly coloured (biscuits will still be soft). Cool on trays for 5-10 minutes. Transfer to a wire rack to cool completely.

Seed Oatcakes

INGREDIENTS

1 cup traditional rolled oats

2/3 cup wholemeal flour

1/2 teaspoon salt

1/4 teaspoon bicarbonate of soda

90g butter, diced

2 egg whites

2 tablespoons sesame seeds

1 tablespoon chia seeds

2 teaspoons poppy seeds

1 teaspoon caraway seeds

2 tablespoons pepitas

EQUIPMENT

Food processor

METHOD

1. Line 2 large baking trays with baking paper.
2. Process oats in a food processor until fine. Add flour, salt and bicarbonate of soda. With motor running, add butter. Process until mixture resembles breadcrumbs. With motor still running, add eggwhites and sesame, chia, poppy and caraway seeds. Process, using the pulse button, until mixture just comes together. Turn onto a lightly floured surface. Knead in pepitas.
3. Divide mixture into two. Roll each piece between floured baking paper into a 20cm circle. Place circles on prepared trays.
4. Preheat oven to 200C or 180C fan-forced. Cut each circle into 8 wedges. Bake for 15 minutes. Cool on tray.

Sugar-Free Blueberry And Banana Yoghurt Cakes

INGREDIENTS

1 cup self-raising flour

1/2 cup wholemeal self-raising flour

1/2 cup Stevia Sweet granules

1 cup reduced-fat plain Greek-style yoghurt

1/2 cup mashed banana (see note)

1/4 cup extra-light olive oil

1 egg

1 cup frozen blueberries

METHOD

1. Preheat oven to 190°C/170°C fan-forced. Grease three 12-hole, 1 1/2 tablespoon-capacity mini muffin pans.

2. Combine flours and stevia together in a bowl. Whisk yoghurt, banana, oil and egg together in a jug. Add to flour mixture. Stir until just combined. Fold through blueberries. Spoon mixture into prepared pan holes.

3. Bake for 12 minutes or until light golden and cakes spring back when lightly pressed. Stand in pan for 5 minutes. Transfer to a wire rack to cool. Serve.

No-Sugar Banana Honey Biscuits

INGREDIENTS

125g butter, chopped, at room temperature

60ml (1/4 cup) honey, plus 1 tablespoon, extra

1 teaspoon vanilla essence

1 egg

1 large ripe banana, well mashed

225g (11/2 cups) plain flour

60ml (1/4 cup) milk

160g spreadable cream cheese

20g (1/3 cup) flaked coconut, toasted

Finely chopped pistachios, to serve (optional)

METHOD

1. Preheat oven to 180C/160C fan forced. Line 2 large baking trays with baking paper. Use electric beaters to beat the butter, honey and vanilla in a bowl until pale and creamy. Add the egg and beat to combine. Beat in the banana (the mixture will appear slightly curdled, but that is okay).

2. Gradually fold in the flour and milk, in alternating batches, until the mixture is smooth and combined. Drop level tablespoons of the mixture onto the trays, allowing room for spreading. Bake for 15 minutes or until springy to touch and light golden. Transfer to a wire rack to cool completely.

3. Stir the cream cheese and extra honey in a small bowl until combined. Spread over the cooled cookies. Sprinkle with coconut and pistachios, if you like.

NOTES

- These soft cookie-cakes will keep, without the topping, for up to 3 days in an airtight container. Keep the topping, covered, in the fridge and add just before serving.

Chocolate Pecan Tart

INGREDIENTS

195g (1 1/2 cups) nutty granola

35g (1/2 cup) shredded coconut

2 fresh dates, pitted

1 tablespoon raw cacao

1 tablespoon black chia seeds

2 tablespoons solidified coconut oil

FILLING

8 fresh dates, pitted

60ml (1/4 cup) maple syrup, plus extra, to serve

1 tablespoon molasses

3 eggs

70g dark chocolate (70% cocoa), chopped

125g (1 cup) pecans

1 tablespoon pepitas

METHOD

1. Preheat the oven to 180C/160C fan forced. Lightly spray a 3cm-deep, 11.5 x 33cm (base measurement) fluted tart tin with removable base with olive oil.

2. Process granola, coconut, dates, cacao, chia and coconut oil in a food processor until mixture resembles fine crumbs. Use damp hands to press mixture into base and sides of prepared tin. Place in the fridge for 15 minutes to chill. Place on a baking tray. Bake for 15 minutes or until crumb is just golden. Use the back of a spoon to gently press down to compact. Set aside to cool.

3. For the filling, place the dates in a large heatproof bowl. Cover with boiling water. Stand for 5 minutes. Drain. Return to the bowl and allow to cool slightly. Add maple syrup and molasses. Use a stick blender to blend for a few seconds, until almost smooth. Add eggs and blend until smooth.

4. Scatter half each of the chocolate and pecans over the tart shell. Pour over the date mixture. Sprinkle with the pepitas and remaining chocolate and pecans. Bake for 25-30 minutes or until the filling is golden and set. Set aside in the pan for 15 minutes. Transfer to a wire rack to cool. Serve the tart drizzled with extra maple syrup.

Printed in Great Britain
by Amazon

40273856R00040